Origin

poems by

Jennifer Hurley

Finishing Line Press
Georgetown, Kentucky

Origin

ACKNOWLEDGMENTS

The Farmer: *Their Buoyant Bodies Respond*
Ruin, The Hunted: *Plath Profiles*
I Watched Him, Our Breakup: *Flying Island*
Sisters, Jack O' Lantern: *Valparaiso Poetry Review*
5:15 AM, First Love: *Etchings*
Slivers, American Summer: *The Cresset*

Publisher: Leah Maines

Editor: Christen Kincaid

Cover Art: Vanessa Hurley, www.noveletchingsphotography.com

Author Photo: Vanessa Hurley, www.noveletchingsphotography.com

Cover Design: Elizabeth Maines

Printed in the USA on acid-free paper.
Order online: www.finishinglinepress.com
            also available on amazon.com

Author inquiries and mail orders:
Finishing Line Press
P. O. Box 1626
Georgetown, Kentucky 40324
U. S. A.

Table of Contents

To my beautiful, remarkable mother

GRANDMOTHER

I watch her body—light, feather-like
center of a séance, floating really. Drifting too
in dim light, I cannot fathom the profound

black that awaits, filling lines of her face.
Shadows settle, permeate her bones, though
still an insignificant weight. To prepare

for this moment I memorized how much she loved
the sky, how she once described it
as *so blue, a newborn boy's first breath.*

Us sunk in overgrown grass, our sweaty
backs relaxed and how she'd touch the tips
of her long fingers to mine, knowing she said

I love you when she really meant to say *oceans.*

GRANDFATHER

I once found a skull on the border of your
struggling corn field. Oatmeal-colored
bone smelled of dirt after rain of deep
earth that bore beneath my fingernails
whenever I buried your Indian pennies
and Nana's rosaries in the banks of the pond.

Based on size and shape I pictured
a puppy, my suntanned hand fit between
rows of peaked teeth, index finger poking
through pretending to touch the dangly
thing that dances at the back of a throat.

I (still) don't know why but you startled
me when rocks shot from beneath
your tires, the gravel road crackled
and dust rose like smoke as if fire
would soon surface. I ran to the other side

clutched the bumpy head to my chest
making it thump against me—a primal
drum. Kneeling behind limp yellowing
plants I opened the mouth again, span
of small jagged points resembling the edge
of a conch shell. Even the air heard you say:

"Hold it close to your ear. Listen for the ocean."

So I did, Grandfather, and I heard the ocean.

THE FARMER

Resting in his electric wheelchair he reads
about telekinetic men bending keys and spoons
women spinning wheels of broken clocks

strains to concentrate on legs hanging limp
still. He needs his fingers to hover and caress
like theirs, to touch without touching.

But each time he's distracted by the soggy fallow
fields his memory suctioning already heavy
feet like thick sticky mud. His wife consoles

him with the same words she whispers to silent
friends: *It could have been caused by a single loose
thread. The books say your mind might develop*

the power to move objects with practice focus.
He knows his old ways are gone and clenches
eyes shut, floats hands over his lap in a circular

motion resembles a maimed marionette whose
puppeteer neglects the missing strings.

LIONS APPARENTLY NOT ENOUGH TO KEEP INTRUDERS OUT
for my grandmother

The only clear detail revealed about her dream
involves lions protecting her home, in craggy
words *enormous majestic golden cats but someone
still broke in.* It's later in the day when even

the sun succumbs to gravity like so many of us,
and she momentarily suspects that I am the thief
the one scheming to sneak inside. She deflects
lingering doubt with polished social graces,

a manner ready to entertain, a custom
of superficial Q&A. Smiling patting my knee:
What's new with you?
Are you coming from work?

Why haven't you stopped by?
I answer each question with matched verve
ready to answer each question, again
and again, my practiced responses words

she doesn't really hear. She occasionally shakes
her head, scrunches her face—interrupts to literally
say: *I have no idea where I am,* her memory
murky moss-green lake water that conceals

everything beyond the surface. I imagine
the wildcats now forgotten extinct their bones
embedded in thick slippery mud a final resting
place with no hope of ever becoming fossils.

JUNCTION

Late, long after I've said prayers, my mother's

home, our family's connecting point, shifts
a vibration that starts at the center of my
spine moments before the freight train's
deep rumble, its distant low note whistle.

Chugging, lugging weight through a pitch
tunnel of night, the honeyed headlight—a tool
of this giant miner—illuminates the way,
so that he can chip away at darkness,

leave vacuous passageways, hollow tubes
that threaten the ceiling. Tonight, I sleep
alone in the bedroom once shared with my
sister, listen for a response to trembling earth,

shaking the cement foundation. A sound similar
to static fills the walls as seams, tugged and tested,
produce a resonant hum, murmur like the high
voltage power lines neighbors swear they can hear

from miles away. The next morning, I wake first,
walk to the quiet kitchen for coffee, notice a slight
rift in the plaster above, a film of bone-white dust
coating the floor. For now, the powder appears

innocuous, as if only flour spilled from a bag.

A WINTER REMISSION

Warmth beckons, even though she knows
mild temperatures betray the season. Dry
eyes scan the deserted Lake Michigan shore
catch glints of wet stones and bright plastic

pieces of broken toys. Petrified wood
lines the vacant beach, resembles
a scattering of old bones. Undaunted she uses
a stranger's femur to help her walk, rubs

her thumb along the curved ridge of a dingy
rib. Moist sand packs beneath bare blue-veined
feet as if brown sugar pressed into a measuring
cup. Each footfall along the water's edge

leaves empty space, digs a shallow grave
refilled again and again by perpetual waves.
In frayed jeans and a threadbare sweatshirt,
her lanky frame treads the air, and she acknowledges

another layer: the confines of a hospital gown,
smudged fingerprints appearing on thin fabric
where bright white used to be. Though worn,
the material sometimes comes to life in the wind:

an uncertain future haunting like a ghost.

RUIN

It would take much more than a lightning-stroke
To create such a ruin.
"The Colossus," Sylvia Plath

Even after my mother passed away Father
ate a runny breakfast at the head of our family's
solid-oak dining table every weekday morning.

The Wednesday afternoon that I found him
dead was no exception. Still sitting dressed
only in bright white underwear and a crewneck
undershirt, his glazed eyes stared at the bronze
knob of a closet door. His cheek stuck in a glob
of golden yolk and slimy whites. Along with
a sticky silver fork, burnt grape-jellied toast
dirtied the floor. And while his hairy arms
hung straight down, thick legs spread
to reveal heavy genitals resting to one side.

I rushed to him, kissed his forehead
as if checking for fever—but his skin
felt so cold that I knew—

and wondered why he wasn't blue—
but more the color of a struggling sun
ray passing through a grey cloudy haze

—and already beginning to crumble.

I WATCHED HIM

I am no source of honey or sweet
but a swarm of domesticated honeybees
buzz wintry-weak in my stomach, their
fuzz bristly wire bottle brushes slowly
scraping away cleaning what's (left) inside.

The emptiness overwhelms early in the day
when the house is so quiet sun yellow warm
I forget to crowd the halls with memories my
son simply hiding, shadows. He had loved
playing in the front yard pines lining the edge

and he knew better at least I thought
I taught him better but he ran into the street
after a dry brown oak leaf bigger than my
hand curling edges teased him along his
fingers reaching out never taking hold. Alone

I watched him from the living room
window not even sure what I was doing
so I'll say drying a glass to prevent
water spots not protesting because I didn't
know I didn't know how far he would

run or how unnaturally his body would
hover legs splayed arms limp socks bloody.

Italicized text from Sylvia Plath's "The Arrival of the Bee Box"

SISTERS

Once, she and I swam together in the Atlantic.
Stepping in from a nearly empty Jersey shore,
our creamy feet flinched from sharp-edged

shells. We had switched bathing suits that day,
each posing in tight, patterned skin of the other.
Neither fit quite right, but we wanted to be

someone different—and the same. With pale
hands locked, we dove into roaring white-capped
waves, an unexpected surge launching us

into an awkward backward somersault. We
actually turned together, moved as one, linked
arms declaring that like Siamese twins, we shared

an umbilical. Looking back, I know the swell
could have mangled us, ripped shoulders
from sockets, bent elbows the wrong way,

forced us to let go. But we surfaced coughing
up salt water, convulsing from laughter,
fingers clenched in an endless, instinctual grip.

5:15 AM

Bare legs tangle and bend filtered moonlight
as if it's a butter-yellow sheet. My younger sister's
two black cats sleep at my feet, huddled into a soft

mound, pointed ears forming peeks of a diminutive
mountain range. Indian Summer air seeps through
screens, though not enough, *not enough,* to move

curtains or push haze of dreams lingering, caught
in dips, valleys of this shadowy room. Tonight,
and just a week ago, I watched her wrist twist

farewell before she disappeared behind the airport's
sliding glass doors. I never guessed the sun
would separate us. But blazing rays had created

a mirror so that I stood waving only to myself.

SLIVERS

I recognize us running freely effortlessly
my brother and I alone, one chasing
the other in the overgrown empty lot
next to our childhood Michigan home.

I can see hastening feet blur as we bolt
between skeletal deprived bushes the height
and breadth of children our age—at the time
imagined foes. Unable to discern faces

I instead recollect shared laughter, the dry
salty taste of open-mouthed breathing, breath short
because we were too young to breathe any
deeper. Separated by just under a year, we

hadn't yet the capacity to fully remember—
images flash only long enough for slivers
of light to appear in the time of idle darkness,
jagged fragments illuminating the measured space

surrounding the frame of a cracked bedroom
door. And, in this dim room, we still sleep.

PRODIGIES
After Daniel Nester's "Prodigies"

He won't leave. I can tell.
I can hear her laughing
low-pitched sighs signs
of an all too familiar habit.
Backing away from my
closed door, I can hear
her hit the glass table
with a shin the irksome
digital melody of an electronic
toy an f-word about my
younger sister's mess. I
burrow beneath my bed, close
my eyes to the light, an earth-
worm wanting to blend
in rich dark prodigal soil.

BACKYARD RECEPTION

Seemingly endless strands
of white Christmas lights
border the backyard. Grass
normally cluttered with rusting
bicycles and grubby dolls
instead shines bright, might
ignite without forecasted
rain, each drop anticipated
to glimmer like a star.

The girl never curls her hair,
leaves it to nature—rats and birds
but today, today, she wears
a floor-length skirt flowing bone
white and is in no way ashamed
of the thin mud line creeping
up her hem, the burnt brown
edge of paper, crumbling.

Wind catches loose tan plastic
bags used to bring casseroles
and dips and they roam, tumbleweeds,
red lettering a discernable
swirl color dancing alongside her
and guests while her blonde
locks flick like flames,
shoot sparks into the sky.

FIRST LOVE

Wet blonde hair, a knotted tangle of dying
vacant lot weeds, covered my eyes as I ran
naked through the house, shriveled feet

slapping wood floors, my whole body blushed
pink from heat after a hot bath. Daddy cast
his voice from the den and hooked me, tugged

at my cheek, reeled me closer, closer, each
time he sang my name. I jumped onto the couch,
crawled into his massive lap, latching short

pudgy arms to his shoulders. Standing, my
five-year-old belly, round and full as if I'd
swallowed a helium balloon, pressed against

his hairy bare chest. Colossal hands rested
at my hips, and I puckered warm lips, kissed him
loud, long, just like the grown-ups on TV.

Marry me! I pleaded in a high-pitched voice,
sliding down his thick torso, his muscular legs,
the way I might slither down carpeted stairs.

THE HUNTED
Inspired by Sylvia Plath's poem, "The Rabbit Catcher"

It is *a place of force—*

So I imagine myself watching the hunted near
a pond in a cold open prairie. Brisk wind echoes
sounds bounding from the end of the world.

I'm bundled in down delicate glass wrapped
for shipping while he sights honking geese
fatty greasy ducks. He can only take three

shots before loading, cocking, shooting—again
each shell exploding in a wide soaking spray.

There is *only one place to get to.*

And this time I'm a rabbit—white nimble
quick, running loose in a backyard booby-trapped
with brambles. Two hard dark nipples peer

from beneath his worn undershirt, a second set
of eyes tracking me. He waits for an enticing
patch of clover, a shock of cottony tops. When

he fires my fur moistens with warm sticky liquid.
The blood clots so fast I never really bleed.

A TENDER AGE

Hugging my pre-school teacher
walking on the street after school
with my mom and the strange yellow
grey glow of the solar eclipse sky
believing that lying would change
my tongue from pure pink to a mossy
lump of foul-smelling green. No more

hugs in kindergarten playing alone
creating construction paper chains (never
long enough) fainting from fever while
singing lead in the Christmas musical.

Chipping my tooth during recess in first
beating up Heather Schlesselman on our
walk home beating up Julie Eberly in
my back yard Dad walking into
the bathroom while I tried to pee
like a boy. Second grade me memorizing

my older brother's prayers before he did
Mrs. Turner's clumped black lashes knowing
I stood different than the other girls discovering
a Lego set in the unplugged avocado-colored
refrigerator in the basement a toy I later
received from Santa Mom blaming me for
finding it even though I wasn't snooping

just making sure nothing had spoiled.

SLINKY

In father's garage, his
wrench clangs against cement
a consistent persistent sound
throughout the day I slip

a slinky on and off the arm
of a favorite doll—little Grace—
my moniker who lost her
dress after the first summer

out in the yard, her hair always
stuck up in strange places as if she
had slept with her head turned
the wrong way we safety-pin

a red shop rag stained with puzzle
pieces of motor oil so that she
has clothes he lets us lay on
the floor with him teaches me

how to walk the slinky open
palms creating stairs between us
encouraging wobbly first steps
trembling like a cold water balloon

or a young girl's exposed breast.

JACK-O'-LANTERN

His love buries me, and he's in a rhythm. Foot
tapping to count signature time, an *Oh, Oh, Oh*
beat—heaving heaped shovels of dirt. Loose
soil, smooth stones, roll across my dull flesh,
slide, bead, seed how lush rain washes a leaf.

Petrified jellyfish surround. Rubbery worms,
hard-backed beetles, weave slimy threads
through limp digits and limbs, pull muddy strands
of morbid loom because it's proper to blanket
the dead. He tells me I will blossom this way.

Fingers and toes burrow, cords of hair plug
into earth, wait for roots to take hold, *hold*. I
imagine a green growth escaping, rising, peeking
through soaked loam: a periscope curling to grant
a 360° view. (Cucumbers cannot grow too close!)

Prickly leaves, flowers yellow and velvet, months
pass before I produce fruit, ripen, start looking
human, again—when skin begins to thicken, ribs
begin to form. Hands twist so many pieces of me
free. Boning knives cut crowns, gutting spoons

scoop sticky insides before they gush like afterbirth.
The unborn will be rinsed, dried, spiced, roasted
on oiled baking sheet. They'll shake, glide across
the silver pan, echo celebratory maracas. Someone
will carve my faces into fright or delight. At night,

a flickering, fugitive light will burn deep inside
until I draw hungry flies, my rinds rot, warp, return.

UNDERWATER

Love makes her believe she can breathe
underwater. She considers the ocean's
edge, bends, grabs gritty handfuls of tan
sand, deep-green seaweed, stuffs pockets
with mottled rocks and shells. Wave after wave,
watery wormholes expose and collapse
time, rush toward their final white bow
how frenzied worshippers charge God.

If she waits for sharp layers of silvery scales
or serrated gills, she'll never make it in, only
flop, flop, flop, slide along the slippery shore.

Lifting her skirt, legs hurdle each swell, navigate
imagined piles of bodies—those unable to evolve.
Dark stains explode on crimson clothes as water
splashes and an undertow circles, skims legs
like a rubbery gray shark. Fingers and feet dig,
form a new hold, determined not to lose her grip
until submerged. When she dances *en pointe*,
graces the undulant floor with an arabesque,
she knows to let go. Floating, flowing,
she opens her mouth, draws in all the sea.

OUR BREAKUP

The afternoon air smells of summer rain, almost
overpowering the reek of bacon and onion fried
early for the German potato salad that you love.

I cook in the morning so the flavors will
grow more distinct after having time to settle
and melt into each other how we once did.

We once did.

Before disappearing for work you used to leave
notes under your coffee mug, the paper stained
brown from little spills—a watercolor

of a white-spotted deer's hide. I always imagined
a fawn, your handwritten words crossed legs
standing for the first time, clumsy wobbly.

But last night when I tried to care for you,
checked mangy fur for ticks and signs of other
disease, your natural camouflage soon hid you

in a thick part of the forest, a forest I continue
to search, now falling asleep cold alone in a pile
of knotty pine branches and slippery sodden leaves.

AMERICAN SUMMER

Kneeling on an oak chair at the kitchen table
Kat pours maple syrup over blueberry pancakes
syrup the color and consistency of motor oil.

In warm morning light, she uses the liquid's
thickness to spell out his name, then writes
the word freedom. *Freedom*—the very first real

breath of it, the very first smell of it—squirms
in her slight frame, a three-ring festival to savor:
as a brown bear balancing on a giant ball roams

the breadth of her stomach, a frantic traveling
flea circus almost escapes her mouth, tightrope
walkers navigate the length of her spine. Shivers.

She thinks about yesterday, a summer day spent
in a wild, idyllic grassy field behind her grandmother's
house, how she had tasted gasoline in his sweat.

With him she drank beer that tasted more like lemonade
and recited a David Baker poem about the Fourth
of July she had to memorize for junior English.

After he had left, she sank into her childhood tree
swing and leaned all the way back, feeling soft
and smooth from the alcohol—and from him. With eyes

closed, the sun made the inside of her eyelids cherry red
as it had many times before. She now knew not to open
them yet, waiting first for a cloud to pass over instead.

LEAVING THE BED

His back rises and falls, while he
      still sleeps, steeps in warm morning sun.

These rays shine onto fair skin and reveal
      a sky embedded in his freckled flesh.

Some form clusters. Others remain separate.
      Together, they resemble a universe brimming

with galaxies, nebulae, constellations, parallel
      worlds. Touching a swirled mass below a shoulder

blade, I wonder where *our love* exists, worry
      he's always beyond reach. Wishing

to unzip and peel away this distance, index
      finger glides down the length of his spine, dipping

in and out of smooth, bony grooves.
      But I expose no real blood. My caress

doesn't wake him any more than
      the bounce created by leaving the bed.

Many of Jennifer's favorite early memories include books: running home from kindergarten so her mother could read aloud from a full-length version of *Snow White and the Seven Dwarfs*; her first-grade teacher's expressive voice while reading Ronald Dahl's *Charlie and the Chocolate Factory* to the class after recess; the author of the Clifford books—Norman Bridwell—visiting her second grade class to discuss his writing and illustrate "The Big Red Dog" right before her eyes.

Also, Jennifer recalls her family, from her mother and aunts to her grandparents, swimming in a sea of books, especially over summer break when a visit to the library generated the same excitement as stopping at a Dairy Queen.

Certainly this nurturing played a role in her desire to write. As early as age thirteen, when asked what she wanted to be when she grew up, Jennifer declared, "An author."

Like so many writers, Jennifer can't remember a time she didn't write; can't remember a time that she didn't appreciate the power of words. She remains amazed by how much a mere word can convey, like love or hate—acceptance or rejection.

She earned a B.S. in Education (Major: English) from Indiana University Bloomington and an M.A. in Liberal Studies (Concentration: English) from Valparaiso University. She pursued her interests in marketing while working in the business sector and has taught English at both the high school and college level. Currently, she works as the Media Specialist for Thomas Jefferson Middle School in Valparaiso, Indiana. Her poetry, fiction, and essays have appeared in various literary publications, including *The Cresset, Etchings, Flying Island, Plath Profiles* (multiple issues), and *Valparaiso Poetry Review* (multiple issues), among others. In addition, one of her poems appeared in the print anthology, *Best of Flying Island, 2014.*

www.ingramcontent.com/pod-product-compliance
Lightning Source LLC
LaVergne TN
LVHW021127080426
835510LV00021B/3351